VINTAGE
TEA PARTY

VINTAGE TEA PARTY

CAROLYN CALDICOTT

PHOTOGRAPHS BY CHRIS CALDICOTT
FOOD STYLING BY CAROLYN CALDICOTT

F

FRANCES LINCOLN LIMITED
PUBLISHERS

Frances Lincoln Limited
4 Torriano Mews
Torriano Avenue
London NW5 2RZ
www.franceslincoln.com

CONTENTS

TEATIME

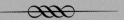

*A*fternoon tea is the quintessential British tradition. At a tea party you enter a nostalgic world of comfort food and vintage style.

This is the story of how afternoon tea developed from its modest beginnings to become a much-loved celebration of indulgent pleasures that include cakes large and small, dainty cucumber sandwiches, scones with jam and cream, crumpets, muffins, and all manner of teatime tipples and assorted teatime paraphernalia.

Forgo the stress of a dinner party and instead gather at home with friends for chat and relaxed afternoons, as enjoyable indoors by the fire in winter as outside in summer sunshine. We show you how to recreate the elegance, tradition and fun of a vintage afternoon tea party with mix-and-match crockery, cutlery, napkins, tablecloths, teapots with cosies and old-fashioned cocktails served in tea cups.

TREASURED TEA-THINGS

Vintage is a word that might be used to describe an antique or something just plain old-fashioned, valued because of its age. A vintage tea party is a chance to rediscover beautiful things, traditions and recipes in a celebration bathed in the rosy glow of nostalgia.

The main thing to remember is that there are no rules: mix and match is the order of the day. Search out old china – rescue it from the back of cupboards or under the stairs or bring it down from the attic. If you can't find a complete tea service simply gather all the china you have and add new pieces with the same feel or colours. Store loose-leaf tea in a caddy and brew it in a teapot, perhaps fitted with a tea cosy (vintage, of course) to keep it warm. The milk jug and sugar bowl need not match but a tea strainer is a must.

Does tea always taste better from a cup? It certainly looks and feels better: holding a cup and saucer almost makes you sit up straighter! Dainty cake plates are the perfect accompaniment for teatime treats but the cake itself, the crowning glory of any table, deserves a special plate or, even better, a cake stand. Little cakes and sandwiches, too, always look their best on a tiered cake stand.

China is only the beginning. There is a plethora of accessories to complete the tea table. I like to buy bundles of knives, forks and spoons of all shapes, sizes and uses when I see them for sale. How about a cake knife for cutting that first slice, and a cake fork to savour eating it? Or a jam spoon to dollop home-made jam, scooped from a cut-glass jam pot, on to a scone? Or a butter knife to spread lashings of butter (taken from a proper butter dish, naturally) on a toasted crumpet? My most treasured find is a domed muffin dish with a secret compartment for hot water to keep the muffins warm.

Of course the table must be covered. If you ever see old linen for sale, snap it up. I have a whole collection of hand-embroidered lace-trimmed tablecloths, but a white sheet is a good substitute (or can be used underneath to help a too-small decorative tablecloth go further). Cover a wooden tray with a tray cloth for cosy teas by the fireside and don't forget the all-important napkin to catch the crumbs.

Finally, flowers – you have to have flowers! Old roses picked fresh from the garden make the perfect tea table decoration, but anything fresh and pretty will add a touch of style. Let your imgination run riot – the important thing is to enjoy it all.

WHERE TO FIND THE VINTAGE LOOK

The first port of call has to be your family. You will be surprised by how many treasures are lurking in the depths of cupboards and drawers; things you may never have seen used. Tea services were always popular wedding presents and I wonder how many were unwrapped, grimaced at, put away and finally given a permanent home in the attic. Or they might have become treasured family heirlooms considered too precious to use (or too much of a bother to get out of the cupboard). These services were made to be used – and finding them gives us a perfect excuse to have a rummage and reminisce.

Once you have exhausted the possibilities at home, it is time to hit the local charity shops, the final destination of many a spring clean, offering an endlessly changing supply of bric-a-brac, linen and cutlery. I have had some amazing finds, from my muffin dish to a complete tea service. Keep looking – remember the perfect teapot could be donated on any day.

Another fun place to find a bargain is a summer fête; there will normally be a bric-a-brac stall selling donated items that might be considered rubbish by someone but are a find to you. And, of course, there will certainly be a cake and refreshment stall to plunder. The dedicated rummager should seek out car-boot and jumble sales where a good deal might be found, after a spot of haggling.

Absolutely my favourite shopping experience has to be a vintage/antiques market or shop – always a treasure trove. There is no need to search here; in fact you may need to show restraint if you don't want to break the bank. Not only is there unlimited choice, but you have the added bonus of enthusiasts at hand to explain the history and use of your purchases.

If all else fails check out the high street. Many kitchen and lifestyle shops sell vintage-style pieces that will mix well with your finds and fill the gaps on the table. Just bear in mind that you're trying to re-create the feeling of 'a past period of quality'. Good hunting.

HOW TO CHEAT IN STYLE

You don't have to be a domestic goddess to have a tea party. As long as the tea ingredients look home-made and are served with vintage style, there are ways to cheat and make life easier.

Women's Institute stalls and farmers' markets are a good secret source of home-made cakes, biscuits, jam and all things delicious. No one will know you haven't been slaving over a hot stove all day. The freezer is also a great aid. Many cakes, muffins, scones, crumpets (the list goes on) freeze very well; if you do bake, next time make double and freeze some to thaw and decorate at a later date and, if you see great cakes for sale, bulk buy and freeze.

It's amazing what you can achieve with a block of shop-bought pastry, some jam, cream and icing sugar. At your local bakery look out for cakes that you can customize. Even supermarkets will sell a plain Victoria sandwich that you can split and fill with lots of whipped cream and strawberries and dust with extra icing sugar.

Shop-bought jam tarts, ready-made pastry cases or even a plain sponge slab, cut into delicate bite-size shapes, can be piped with a swirl of whipped cream (flavoured with seeds scraped from a vanilla pod) and topped with redcurrants or raspberries. You can buy brandy snaps and keep them in the cupboard for weeks, ready to fill with flavoured whipped cream. When summer fruit is plentiful, you can make a deliciously simple sweet by layering the cooked fruit with shop-bought vanilla custard and whipped cream in a pretty glass (and you can always freeze the extra cooked fruit).

Shop-bought muffins, currant buns and crumpets still look wonderful toasted and covered in butter. Even the most inexperienced cook can make a sandwich: just remove the crusts and cut into dainty shapes. However, never compromise on jam: if you don't have a home-made jar, buy the best available, and always check the fruit-to-sugar content on the back of the label (the fruit should always be higher).

Finally, it is all about presentation: serve your cake creations on vintage tea-things and lace-edged paper doilies for maximum impact.

THE START OF THE AFFAIR

Britain's love affair with tea began in the mid-seventeenth century when green tea first arrived on merchant ships from China. However, like many passions it was promptly banned by the puritan Cromwell as being far too decadent, despite counterclaims that it was good for health.

Luckily his successor, Charles II, became a convert to the pleasures of a good cuppa when his new wife, Catherine of Braganza, already a confirmed tea addict, brought a chest of tea to England as part of her dowry. The royal court instantly fell for the charms of green tea, drunk in the oriental style, without milk, from little handleless cups. The wealthy elite, keen to keep up with the new fashion and rich enough to afford it, soon followed suit. At home, being so precious (and expensive), tea was kept in a locked caddy with the mistress of the house being the sole keeper of the key.

Soon coffee shops, dealers in china and even chemists (as tea was still considered to be good for one's health) were offering a chance to sample the delicious brew, but only at a high cost. High taxation led to a flourishing trade in smuggled tea and dealers regularly mixed the valuable commodity with twigs and leaves. Even the wealthy were not averse to using tea leaves twice and a brisk trade in used leaves became commonplace and enabled the less fortunate to have their first sip. What they did not realize was that the used leaves were often mixed with sheep's dung or poisonous copper carbonate to maintain the correct colour of brewed tea.

By the late eighteenth century the government had decided to tackle tea-smuggling. In 1784 the whopping 119% tax on tea was reduced to a more reasonable 12.5%, thereby ending the illegal trade overnight and bringing affordable unadulterated tea to the masses.

The East India Company, eager to break China's world monopoly on the tea trade, established tea plantations in India and Sri Lanka and by the mid-nineteenth century cheaper tea from Darjeeling, Assam and Ceylon was flooding the market. A new passion for tea served with milk (added perhaps to modify the flavour of bitter tannins in the stronger black tea) seized the British public.

In a bid to oust beer's popularity and create a more sober society, the Temperance movement promoted tea made with boiling water as a safe way to drink water. Their hopes were realized as tea took the country by storm to become the great national drink we know and love today.

HOW TEATIME BEGAN

Little did Anna, Duchess of Bedford, realize that when she succumbed to a late afternoon 'sinking feeling' one day in 1840 and asked for tea, bread, butter and cake to be sent to her private rooms at her stately home, Woburn Abbey, she was starting a new craze. Breakfast at the time was served early and dinner late. Both were lavish affairs but little attention was given to the light midday meal known as luncheon (often eaten buffet style with no servants in attendance), so by 4 o'clock it was not surprising that Anna was more than a little hungry.

Fortified by her tasty repast she soon decided to share the experience with her lady friends by sending out invitations for 'Tea and a walk in the fields'. On returning to London for the Season, Anna continued her afternoon ritual, taking tea in the drawing room with invited friends and, as she was lady-in-waiting to and life-long friend of Queen Victoria, afternoon tea became fashionable.

Afternoon tea was now official, served between 4 and 5 o'clock in the drawing room on low tables in front of the sofa, and followed by a promenade in Hyde Park. What to wear? Well, the tea gown of course, designed in silk and chiffon to be as light and delicate as the cakes themselves, and edged with lace and embroidery.

The great china factories such as Spode, Minton and Wedgwood expanded their tea-service repertoire to include cake plates, tiered cake stands, bread and butter plates, lavish teapots, cream jugs and more. Bone china was preferred: white, translucent and hand-painted to match the new fashions, it also kept the tea hotter for longer. From Sheffield a whole new array of cutlery emerged.

New recipes for glamorous cakes were invented to adorn the table and soon afternoon tea became an orgy of pleasures, the table heavy with the weight of extravagant cakes, lavish tea services and ornate silver teapots. Amongst all this excess, etiquette demanded that conversation be kept light and lady-like. Whole books were dedicated to instructing the hostess how to behave, thereby firmly establishing the ritual of afternoon tea in polite society.

FROM DRAWING ROOM TO TEAROOM

The new craze spread quickly. The Aerated Bread Company, famous for their so-called hygienic yeast-free bread, became pioneers when in 1864 a London-based manageress, in a bid to boost takings, had the idea of serving tea along with their baked goods. The new tearoom was a success, as an avalanche of respectable ladies took advantage of being able to eat out unescorted without risking their reputations.

Like all successful ideas it was quickly copied and tearooms became the fashion, with department stores offering afternoon tea with musical accompaniment to entertain their genteel customers. Elegance was all, with hats and gloves a must. By the end of the nineteenth century J. Lyons had opened its famous tearooms, with uniformed waitresses, affectionately known as 'nippies', serving tea to the public in stylish surroundings.

By the early twentieth century grand hotels, with a long tradition of serving afternoon tea, had devised the Tea Dance: an orchestra would play light music whilst ladies in delicate, diaphanous dresses would waltz away the late afternoon with their partners, taking frequent breaks to refresh themselves with the all-important cup of tea and cake. It became the perfect opportunity to meet members of the opposite sex.

CHOOSING YOUR TEA

'Put the kettle on,' those immortal words! A cup of tea wakes us in the morning, calms us in the evening, picks us up in the afternoon and celebrates good news.

Tea should be treated like a fine wine, whose personality is decided by many factors. Interestingly, all tea comes from varieties of the same bush, *Camellia sinensis*. It is grown at high altitudes, and only the top two leaves and a bud are picked from the new growth that the plant puts on every one to two weeks.

Where and when it is picked is important but the most crucial factor to a tea's character is fermentation. Green tea is unfermented: the leaves are simply dried after picking, thus preventing oxidization and preserving the green colour and grassy taste. To enjoy the flavour to the maximum, always serve green tea unadulterated.

Black tea, drunk by the gallon in Britain, is the product of fermentation: the leaves are wilted then rolled in a machine to bruise them and release the enzymes responsible for the process of oxidization. The leaves are then left to ferment and finally dried, giving them the characteristic black colour. Enjoy served with a little milk or lemon.

Oolong tea gives you the best of both worlds. It is only partially fermented, to create a delicate-tasting tea that can be drunk either with milk or lemon or on its own.

On the next pages I have selected a few of my favourites to help you choose from the many types of tea. You might also like to offer a choice to your guests.

FROM INDIA

Assam tea
This strong black tea with its malty flavour is a good everyday tea.

Darjeeling tea
From the foothills of the Himalayas and often called the champagne of tea as it has a light, delicate flavour.

Nilgiri tea
From the Malabar hills of south India this is a medium-strength black tea perfect with dainty cakes.

FROM CHINA

Keemun tea
This black tea from the Huangshan Mountains is said by the Chinese to have 'the fragrance of an orchid'. Serve with or without a little milk.

Formosa oolong
This is one of the most highly treasured teas from China; semi-fermented, it is best taken without milk, so that you can to enjoy the characteristic peach-blossom flavour. Look out for oolong scented with rose petals – it is delicious served with meringues.

Lapsang souchong
This is a distinctive smoky-tasting robust black tea; though it is not to everyone's taste, many love it, either with or without milk.

Green tea

There are many grades of green tea from China and the most commonly known is gunpowder – little pellets of rolled leaves that produce a sharp-tasting pale tea. Try one of the more expensive green teas such as lung ching for a softer cleaner taste or jasmine tea scented with jasmine flowers. Never serve with milk.

FROM SRI LANKA

Ceylon tea

A lovely golden, mild-flavoured black tea.

FROM JAPAN

Try grassy light green teas such as **bancha tea** or splash out on **matcha tea**, as used in the traditional tea ceremony.

FROM AFRICA

Kenya tea

A medium-strength black tea, perfect for afternoon tea.

BLENDED TEA

Earl Grey

A scented blend of black China and Darjeeling teas flavoured with bergamot oil, popular served in the afternoon with either lemon or a little milk.

Historically, to add a theatrical note and allow the hostess to show off her tea-mixing skills, tea was made at the table. The tea caddy would be unlocked to reveal the precious tea – usually several varieties which would then be mixed in a special bowl to achieve the perfect blend. An ornate silver kettle kept on the table at a constant simmer ensured the freshest possible tea. To prevent the tea becoming stewed a second warmed pot was often at hand to pour it into when it had reached the required brewing time.

THE QUESTION OF MILK

Some say we add milk to stop the heat of boiling water breaking the fine china cups, others that it is to make the drink more tasty by neutralizing the tannin in the tea. Like the question of milk first or last, it is a matter of personal taste. What follows is my preference.

THE PERFECT CUP OF TEA

Forget tea bags. Loose tea is essential for the perfect brew. And, of course, you should never serve tea in a mug.

Pour fresh water into an empty limescale-free kettle and bring to the boil, making sure the water does not boil for too long, as the oxygen in the water is needed for the best taste. The longer the kettle boils the less oxygen will remain in the water.

Pour a little boiling water into the teapot and then discard after a good swirl around the pot.

Add your tea, allowing one spoon per person and one for the pot, and pour over the boiled water.

Cover the pot with a cosy and allow to brew for 3 to 5 minutes depending on how strong you like your tea.

Pour a little cold milk into a cup then add the hot tea, pouring through a strainer.

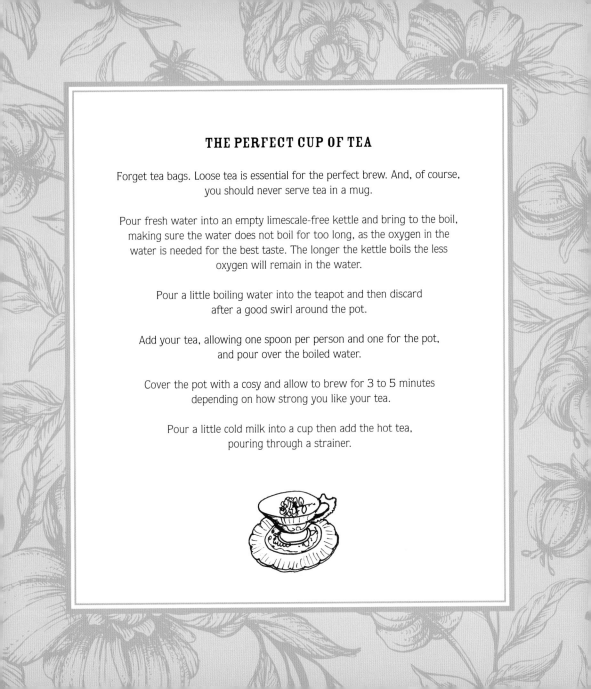

THE HISTORY OF THE SANDWICH

The 4th Earl of Sandwich is said to have inadvertently invented the great British snack in the mid-eighteenth century. The story goes that while at the gaming table he asked for some cold meat to be served between two pieces of bread (so as not to make his hands, and hence his cards, greasy). Other gentlemen followed suit by asking for the 'same as Sandwich'.

Inevitably the sandwich became incorporated into the new craze for afternoon tea, although the original style of hunks of meat inside chunks of bread was replaced with more refined versions. Afternoon-tea sandwiches are as elegant as the event itself, bite-sized and crust-free with light and tasty fillings, since it's imperative to leave enough room for all the sweet treats on offer.

However, when sandwiches are served as high tea, which takes the place of the evening meal, they can be hearty affairs full of cold cuts and strong cheese with pickle.

ALL SHAPES AND SIZES

You can be as creative as you like as long as you remove the crusts for afternoon tea. Use different types of bread to give a choice of texture, flavour and colour on the table. Sandwich flags are not only decorative but also a convenient way to describe the sandwich filling to your guests.

A classic is the **finger sandwich**: cut each round into four horizontal finger shapes. Little squares and triangles are also traditional, while a fun option is to use pastry cutters to make all manner of shapes from hearts to diamonds. Or you could try the **rolled sandwich**: cut the crusts off slices of bread from a large sandwich loaf, flatten each slice with a rolling pin, spread with butter and a smooth or sticky sandwich filling, and roll tightly like a Swiss roll; finally trim the ends and cut in half to make dainty rolls or thinly slice the roll to make pinwheels.

Sandwiches need to be made as near to serving as possible to taste their best. Store in a sealed container or cover with a clean damp cloth until you are ready to eat.

TEATIME TIPPLES

Who says teatime has to be temperate?

By the time the vogue for afternoon tea had reached its heady heights, stronger drinks had been incorporated into its list of pleasures; claret cup and champagne cup (see page 59) were ladled from ornate bowls into punch glasses. Follow the Victorians' example and let your tea party go with a swing.

Champagne afternoon tea is a luxurious pleasure any time. Or you could serve the 1920s flappers' favourite, Earl Grey tea laced with gin and lemon (see page 100), or warm up a cold winter's afternoon with a hot tea toddy (see page 82) at the fireside.

PRESERVES

*T*here is nothing quite like a generous spoon of home-made fruit preserve on a warm scone, raspberry jam oozing from a light sponge cake or lemon curd bubbling in a tart hot from the oven. Easy, cheap and terribly satisfying to make, jam offers a chance to create something a bit different.

Collect used jam jars and sterilize either by placing in the oven when cold and heating to 100°C/210°F/gas mark ¼, or carefully swilling with a little boiling water. Cover your jam with little waxed paper circles before sealing. Decorate by covering the lid with pretty doilies or patterned paper circles; there are lots of great options for sale in good kitchen shops or department stores. Of course there is always the cheat's option of buying home-made jam whenever you see it for sale and storing it in a cool place until required.

To serve, spoon into a jam pot or cut-glass dish with its own special jam spoon.

DAMSON OR PLUM JAM

This recipe works well for plums, but it is worth searching out the more unusual and old-fashioned damson. Good greengrocers usually stock them in late summer. I always buy mine from the local Women's Institute stall.

MAKES ABOUT 1.3kg/3lb
900g/2lb damsons or plums
380ml/2/3 pint water
800g/1lb 12oz granulated sugar

1. Remove any stalks and wash the fruit.
2. Place in a heavy-bottomed pan along with the water and bring to the boil, reduce heat and simmer until the fruit is quite soft, squashing it against the side of the pan to encourage the fruit to break down.
3. Remove the pan from the heat and add the sugar, stirring until it has all dissolved.
4. Return the pan to the heat and bring back to the boil for 10 minutes, then reduce heat to a simmer again.
5. By now the stones of the fruit will be rising to the surface; remove them with a slotted spoon. Keep the jam at a simmer to encourage the stones to rise.
6. By the time all stones are removed the jam should have reached setting point. Test by placing a teaspoon of jam on a chilled saucer: if the surface of the jam wrinkles when pushed it is ready; if not, continue to simmer and test again.
7. Ladle into clean, warm, sterilized jars, cover with a waxed paper disc and seal with a lid immediately.

FORAGER'S ELDERBERRY AND BLACKBERRY JAM

In late summer the elder tree is heavy with bunches of tiny deep-purple berries crying out to be made into jam. Mix with blackberries to create the perfect jam for tea.
The quantity of jam you make is dependent on how many berries you pick.

Equal quantities of elderberries and blackberries
350g/12oz granulated sugar per 450g/1lb pound of fruit

1. Remove any stalks from the blackberries and wash thoroughly. Wash the elderberries whilst still on the stalk then remove the berries by dragging the stalks through the prongs of a fork.
2. Place the berries in a heavy-bottomed saucepan, bring the fruit to simmer point and cook for 15 minutes.
3. Stir in the granulated sugar until dissolved, then bring to a brisk boil for 20 minutes; test the setting point (as described in the recipe opposite); if still a little runny, boil for a further few minutes.
4. Remove from the heat and ladle into sterilized jars; cover with a waxed paper disc and seal immediately.

LEMON CURD

Creamy, light and zesty, lemon curd is so versatile: dollop on warm scones on a hot summer's day, bake in tarts for a hearty high tea or sandwich with cream between a light sponge.

My mother always made lemon curd in a stone jar that I have now inherited. It's worth keeping an eye out for these jars as they make the best lemon curd containers.

MAKES ABOUT 450g/1lb
3 unwaxed lemons
110g/4oz butter, diced
225g/8oz caster sugar
3 large free-range eggs, beaten

1. Grate the zest of the lemons, then squeeze the juice.
2. Place the butter in a heatproof bowl over a pan of simmering water; when melted gradually stir in the caster sugar and beaten egg.
3. Add the lemon zest and juice and stir regularly until the curd thickens and coats the back of a spoon.
4. Pour into a stone jar and simply cover with a waxed paper disc and a circle of greaseproof paper secured with a rubber band; alternatively pour into sterilized jam jars, cover with a waxed paper disc and seal with a lid. Allow to cool and thicken overnight, then store in the fridge.

ROSE PETAL JAM

A really old-fashioned jam rarely seen anymore, rose petal jam is delicious spread on to buttered fresh bread. I make it when the petals of my roses are quite loose, as I cannot bear to destroy perfect roses. It is best to pick the petals in the morning from heavily scented pesticide-free roses. Make in small batches, as it does not have a very long shelf life.

MAKES ABOUT 450g/1lb
225g/8oz rose petals
450g/1lb jam sugar
1 litre/2 pints water
juice of 2 lemons

1. Pick the petals, cutting off the base of each leaf as you go; if the leaves are large, tear them into smaller pieces.
2. Place the petals in a plastic tub with a well-fitting lid. Sprinkle with half the sugar, making sure you cover all of the petals; seal the tub and leave overnight to draw out the perfume.
3. Pour the water, remaining sugar and lemon juice into a saucepan, place on a low heat and stir the liquid constantly until the sugar has completely dissolved.
4. Stir in the rose petals and simmer for 25 minutes, then boil rapidly for 5 minutes. The jam will thicken, but it does not respond to testing its thickness on a cold saucer.
5. Ladle into small warm sterilized jam jars. Cover with waxed jam covers and seal immediately.

RASPBERRY JAM

Raspberries make a delicate luxurious jam, perfect for cakes. They don't contain a lot of pectin so it's best to use jam sugar and a little lemon juice to help it set.

Follow the recipe for elderberry and blackberry jam (see page 35), cooking the raspberries initially for only 8 minutes, then add jam sugar and the juice of one lemon per 450g/1lb of fruit, boil until setting point is reached, and pot in the usual way.

STRAWBERRY AND CHAMPAGNE JAM

The most luxurious of jams, not too firmly set, strawberry and champagne jam is superb with scones. The recipe uses champagne but you can substitute any dry sparkling white or rosé wine quite happily – and drink up the leftovers!

MAKES ABOUT 900g/2lb
450g/1lb ripe strawberries, washed hulled and cut into quarters
375g/12oz jam sugar
175ml/⅓ pint champagne
4 tablespoons freshly squeezed lemon juice

1. In a heavy-bottomed pan combine the strawberries, jam sugar and champagne; stir over a low heat until the sugar has dissolved.
2. Add the lemon juice and gently simmer for 20 minutes, then bring to a rapid boil for 5 minutes.
3. Test the setting point as described on page 34, then allow the jam to sit for 15 minutes in the pan to solidify a little; this will prevent the fruit from floating to the top when it's in the jar.
4. Ladle the jam into clean, warm sterilized jars. Cover with wax discs and seal immediately. The jam sets as it cools, and I also find it tends to set a little more over the next 24 hours.

TEA IN THE DRAWING ROOM

*A*fternoon tea in the drawing room was also known as low tea, as the hostess would serve tea from a low table conveniently placed in front of the sofa or low-sided arm chair. Guests, elegantly dressed in tea gowns, would gather round to share gossip and light conversation. The exquisite delicacies on offer would be strictly kept to bite size (since a lavish dinner would be taken later). At the height of the fashion for afternoon tea, several invitations a day came for popular ladies, who would often while away the afternoon hopping from one tea party to the next.

You can re-create the elegance of a traditional drawing-room tea. Take out your best china to display dainty smoked salmon and expertly rolled pinwheel sandwiches. Only a tiered cake stand will do justice to delicate tarts, millefeuilles and light-as-air lemon drops.

A tablecloth is a must, laid with a host of pretty teatime paraphernalia. Set the mood with doilies, sandwich flags and linen napkins, and decorate with flowers.

Be the hostess with the mostest, presiding over the party from the sofa serving Darjeeling, the champagne of tea, or let the party swing with claret cup (see page 59) or Earl Grey with lemon, spiked with a healthy measure of gin (see page 100).

SMOKED SALMON AND CREAM CHEESE SANDWICHES

Mix cream cheese with a squeeze of lemon juice, a pinch of cayenne pepper, finely chopped chives and freshly ground black pepper. Spread on to buttered brown bread and layer with good quality smoked salmon; cover with another buttered slice, cut away the crusts and cut into dainty squares, or roll as described on page 28.

EGG AND CRESS SANDWICHES

My personal favourite, egg and cress sandwiches are synonymous with afternoon tea and simple to make.

Hard boil free-range eggs, cooling in cold water to avoid an ugly dark ring around the yolk. Peel the eggs and crush with a fork in a bowl, add mayonnaise, salt and pepper to taste and mix well. Spread on to buttered bread, sprinkle with cress and top with buttered bread; gently press together and cut away the crusts. Roll (see page 28) or cut into the desired shape for your plate.

LEMON DROPS

Stunning little bite-size cakes decorated with lemon curd, whipped cream and the dramatic Cape gooseberry (physalis).

MAKES ABOUT 12 CAKES
1 light sponge cake (see page 58)
lemon curd (see page 38)
275ml/½ pint double cream, whipped until thick
caster sugar
Cape gooseberries (physalis), with leaves folded back and twisted a little so they stand upright

1. Make a Genoese cake as described in the recipe on page 58.
2. Using a 5cm/2in round metal pastry cutter cut into 12 little cakes.
3. Cut each cake in half and spread with lemon curd, top with whipped double cream and sandwich together.
4. Sprinkle with caster sugar, top with a little piped whipped double cream and place a prepared Cape gooseberry on top. Serve as soon as possible.

English macaroons were created in the eighteenth century as a tasty mid-morning accompaniment to a glass of wine. Characterized by their honey colour and almond topping they are quite different from their French namesakes. They proved so popular that they were soon adorning puddings such as trifle and syllabub and, of course, the tea table.

ENGLISH MACAROONS

These light, sweet almond biscuits are a perfect complement to afternoon tea. Traditionally they are baked on rice paper; however, if this is hard to find simply grease the baking tray instead.

MAKES ABOUT 18

2 large free-range egg whites
225g/8oz caster sugar
110g/4oz ground almonds

25g/1oz rice flour
1 teaspoon orange flower water
split blanched almonds

1. Preheat the oven to 180°C/350°F/gas mark 4.
2. Line 2 baking trays with rice paper.
3. Whisk the egg whites until fairly stiff, then gradually whisk in the sugar.
4. Fold in the ground almonds, rice flour and orange flower water.
5. Spoon teaspoonfuls of the mixture on to the prepared baking trays, allowing enough room for each biscuit to spread, and then top each macaroon with a split blanched almond.
6. Bake in the preheated oven for 20 to 25 minutes, until pale golden in colour.
7. Remove from the oven and allow to cool, then cut around each biscuit so that it is lined with rice paper.

CHOCOLATE

Chocolate, brought to Europe from Mexico by the Spanish conquistadores, reached Britain in the seventeenth century. First advertised in London as 'an excellent drink, which cures the body and mind', chocolate was heated with milk and sugar and frothed with a whisk to serve. Chocolate houses quickly spread across the city, becoming the fashionable venue in which to drink the new delicacy. Precursors of the teahouse, chocolate houses became hotbeds of radical political debate and intrigue.

By the end of the eighteenth century chocolate had entered recipes for desserts, cakes and even savoury dishes. The new technique of removing cocoa butter from the crushed bean produced cocoa (which was more easily mixed with milk); moreover, when the extracted cocoa butter was mixed with ground cocoa beans and sugar it led to the creation of the chocolate bar. This new exotic delight was considered such a delicacy that it would be proudly displayed at the centre of the tea table under a glass dome.

CHOCOLATE MERINGUE CAKE

This is simply the best chocolate cake you will ever taste. Make it with good dark chocolate, and serve with strawberries and whipped cream.

225g/8oz unsalted butter, plus a little extra to grease the cake tin
200g/7oz good dark chocolate, broken into pieces
6 medium free-range eggs, separated
200g/7oz caster sugar
icing sugar, for dusting the finished cake
275 ml/½ pint double cream, whisked until thick
strawberries, washed, hulled and cut in half

1. Preheat the oven to 190°C/375°F/gas mark 5 and grease a clip-release 23cm/9in loose-bottomed cake tin.
2. Melt the chocolate and butter in a bowl over a simmering pan of water. Remove from the heat and stir together until well mixed.
3. Whisk the egg whites until very stiff, then gradually whisk in the sugar until the mixture looks glossy, and finally whisk in the egg yolks until the mixture is creamy.
4. Using a metal spoon quickly combine the chocolate butter sauce with the cake mixture and pour into the prepared cake tin.
5. Bake for 1 hour on the middle shelf of the oven; the cake will rise up, then sink back when removed from the oven, giving it its characteristic appearance.
6. Allow to cool, remove the outer ring of the cake tin, but don't even try to take the delicate cake off its base. Dust with icing sugar and decorate with the whipped cream and strawberries.

As afternoon tea grew more popular, inspiration was sought from the great patisserie chefs of France and millefeuille, 'thousand-leaf', pastry is a perfect example of this.

RASPBERRY MILLEFEUILLES

This light flaky patisserie is a real show stopper; sandwiched with raspberry jam and whisked double cream and topped with glacé icing and raspberries, it looks complicated but is actually very easy to prepare if you buy the puff pastry.

MAKES ABOUT 12

250g/9oz puff pastry
110g/4oz icing sugar
seedless raspberry jam

275ml/½ pint double cream, whipped
raspberries to decorate

1. Preheat the oven to 230°C/450°F/gas mark 8.
2. Roll out the puff pastry on a lightly floured surface until 3mm/⅛in thick and cut circles of pastry, using a 6cm/2½in-diameter round pastry cutter.
3. Prick the surface of each round repeatedly with a fork to ensure the pastry rises evenly; place on a non-stick baking tray with enough room to spread.
4. Bake in the oven for 10–15 minutes until crisp and golden brown.
5. Remove from the oven and cool on a cake rack.
6. Lightly flatten each pastry a little, with your hand, and then cut in half with a thin sharp knife.
7. Add water to the icing sugar a little at a time until the glacé icing is smooth and thick enough to coat the back of a spoon.
8. Ice the lid of each pastry and put to one side until set enough to handle.
9. Assemble each millefeuille by spreading the pastry base with a little raspberry jam, followed by piped whipped double cream, and rest the iced lid on top. Pipe a little cream on the centre of the icing and finally decorate with a raspberry. Once assembled serve as soon as possible.

Shortbread may have evolved from the sixteenth-century short cakes served at funerals, though this is disputed. However, its origins are firmly agreed to be Scottish.

SHORTBREAD BISCUITS

Delicate, crumbly and sprinkled with caster sugar, shortbread must be handled as little as possible for the perfect texture. I often add a little dried lavender for an untraditional twist

MAKES ABOUT 12 BISCUITS
175g/6oz plain flour
pinch of salt
50g/2oz caster sugar
110g/4oz soft butter
caster sugar for dusting

1. Preheat the oven to 180°C/350°F/gas mark 4.
2. Sift the flour and salt together into a mixing bowl, then stir in the sugar.
3. Cut the butter into small cubes and gently rub into the flour mixture until a dough forms.
4. Roll out on to a lightly floured surface until about ½cm/¼in thick.
5. Cut into 6cm/2½in rounds and place on a non-stick baking tray.
6. Bake on the middle shelf of the oven for 15–20 minutes; the biscuits should be a pale buttery colour.
7. Remove from the oven and sprinkle with caster sugar while still warm, then cool on a cake rack.

GENOESE CAKE

This light and springy classic sponge forms the perfect base for several cakes, for example a Swiss roll (see page 123), cut into petite rounds for lemon drops (see page 46), sandwiched with jam and cream or simply iced.

3 large free-range eggs
110g/4oz caster sugar

110g/4oz self-raising flour, sifted
2 tablespoons melted butter

1. Preheat the oven to 200°C/400°F/gas mark 6.
2. Line an 18cm/7in x 28cm/11in (approx.) oblong tin with greaseproof paper, cutting the corners diagonally so they sit snugly in the tin. Brush with a little of the melted butter.
3. In a mixing bowl whisk the eggs and sugar for about 10 minutes until thick and creamy and the whisk leaves a trail when lifted.
4. Fold in the sifted flour and melted butter to make a smooth thick batter.
5. Pour into the prepared cake tin and bake for 10 minutes until golden and firm to touch.
6. Allow to cool a little, then carefully turn out of the tin and remove the greaseproof paper.

CLARET CUP

Claret cup was the Victorians' favourite afternoon tea cocktail.

1 bottle of claret or red wine
1 liqueur glass sherry
2 liqueur glasses brandy
juice of a lemon
strip of peel cut from
   an orange and a lemon

½ teaspoon grated nutmeg
3 tablespoons caster sugar
500ml/1 pint soda water
crushed ice
sprigs of borage or strips
   of cucumber peel to garnish

Combine all the ingredients in a large bowl, ladle into punch glasses and garnish.

CHAMPAGNE CUP

How about the more luxurious champagne version?

1 bottle champagne
2 liqueur glasses brandy
2 tablespoons caster sugar

400ml/¾ pint soda water
crushed ice
strips of cucumber peel to garnish

Combine all the ingredients in a jug and pour into garnished glasses immediately.

Sloes are the astringent fruit of the blackthorn tree. Round and deep purple in colour, they are picked in autumn when soft to the touch and plentiful.

Every Christmas my grandmother would proudly bring out the treasured bottle of sloe gin that we had all helped to make by collecting wild sloes from the hedgerows, then sharing the tedious job of pricking the fruit with the prongs of a fork. I now make the task much easier by placing the sloes in the freezer overnight, which has the dual effect of splitting the skins and breaking down the sugar in the sloes.

SLOE GIN WITH CHAMPAGNE

Sloe gin is a superlative companion to champagne and together they make a lovely old-fashioned cocktail for a tea party. Pour a little gin into the bottom of a champagne glass, then top with champagne or any dry sparkling white wine.

TO MAKE THE SLOE GIN
454g/1lb washed sloes
175g/6oz white granulated sugar
75ml bottle gin

2 vanilla pods, split
sterilized Kilner jar (roughly 2litre/4lb-
capacity for this amount of fruit)

1. Either prick the sloes with a fork, a fistful at a time, or take the easier option of putting them in the freezer overnight.
2. Pour the sugar into the Kilner jar, follow with the sloes and the seeds scraped from the split vanilla pods, and finally pour over the gin.
3. Seal and store in a cool dark place for 3 months, turning every few days to mix the sugar, sloes and gin.
4. After 3 months strain the gin from the fruit and pour into sterilized bottles. You can drink it straight away but it is best to leave it for at least a further 3 months.

HIGH TEA

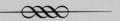

*H*igh tea, unlike the light and elegant afternoon tea, is hearty, rustic and substantial, and enjoyed by all the family. Traditionally served at the end of the working day, at the later hour of 6 o'clock, high tea replaced dinner and subsequently became a much more generous meal.

Without the risk of ruining one's appetite for later, guests felt free to indulge themselves with the abundant pleasures on offer. Salad, toast, muffins, sides of ham, chunks of cheese, pickles and meat pies characterized the event. Whisky- or rum-laced tea often encouraged free-flowing conversation. Ladies sat square to the table to partake, whilst gentlemen gathered round, noisily discussing the day's events, with cup on the table, plate on the knee and a large hanky to catch the crumbs.

For high tea, serve bubbling hot cheesy Welsh rarebit, boiled eggs with bread and salty butter, beef and horseradish sandwiches, carved pork and ham pies, salad and crumpets. Rich fruity Eccles cakes, homely coffee and walnut cake, jam tarts and thick slices of old-fashioned seed cake can follow. All washed down with a constant supply of full-bodied Assam tea.

Don't worry about a tablecloth: simply lay the table with chunky china, cover the pot with a knitted tea cosy and eat informally around the table.

WELSH RAREBIT

Who can resist melted cheese on toast . . . ?

SERVES 4

225g/8oz strong Cheddar cheese, grated
1 tablespoon butter
1 teaspoon mustard powder
2 teaspoons plain flour

2 teaspoons Worcestershire sauce
4 tablespoons beer (or milk for the teetotal)
black pepper to taste
4 thick slices of bread, crusts and all

Combine the cheese, butter, mustard, flour and Worcestershire sauce in a pan and gently warm until melted, gradually adding the beer. Stir regularly to ensure a smooth texture, and add black pepper to taste.

Toast the bread on one side, spread the cheese on the untoasted side and place under a hot grill until bubbling and golden. Serve immediately.

POTTED SALMON

A wonderful old-fashioned recipe, perfect for filling rolled sandwiches or spreading on hot buttered toast.

200g/7oz cooked or tinned salmon, skin and bones removed
40g/1½oz melted butter
a good pinch of ground mace
freshly ground black pepper and salt to taste

Blend all the ingredients together until a smooth paste forms, keeping back a little of the butter to pour on top of the paste to form a seal if storing in the fridge.

HIGH TEA SANDWICHES

Ham and English mustard, rare roast beef and horseradish, cheddar cheese and pickle are all superb fillings for the more substantial high tea sandwich.

CRUMPETS

Nothing beats a home-made crumpet; shop-bought crumpets only hint at how utterly delicious they are. The crisp outside brilliantly balances the soft honeycomb centre, the perfect receptacle for melted butter on its own. For a savoury taste spread them with Marmite or melted cheese, or sweeten them with home-made jam or honey.

You will need crumpet rings for this recipe; if these are hard to find, egg rings are just as good or you could even use heart-shaped metal pastry cutters.

MAKES 10

150ml/¼ pint full-fat milk
150ml/¼ pint water
1 level teaspoon caster sugar
1 dessertspoon dried yeast
110g/4oz strong white flour

110g/4oz plain flour
½ teaspoon salt
¼ teaspoon bicarbonate of soda
1 tablespoon warm water
1 tablespoon sunflower oil

1. Gently warm the milk and water together in a saucepan until hand hot, then remove from the heat.
2. Stir in the sugar, yeast and oil until dissolved; set to one side for 15 minutes, until the mixture is very frothy.
3. Meanwhile sift the flours and salt into a mixing bowl and make a well in the centre.
4. Pour the milk mixture into the well and stir thoroughly until the batter is completely smooth.
5. Cover with a clean tea towel and leave in a warm place for 45 minutes. Bubbles will cover the surface of the batter.
6. Dissolve the bicarbonate of soda in the tablespoon of warm water and stir into the batter, cover and leave for a further 45 minutes.
7. Oil 3 crumpet rings and a heavy frying pan or griddle with a little sunflower oil; put the rings on top of the pan and heat the pan to a moderate temperature.
8. Three-quarter fill each ring with batter and gently cook for about 8 minutes until holes form on the surface and the batter is set. If bubbles don't form add a little more warm water to the batter.

9. Remove the rings and turn the crumpets over to cook for a further 4 minutes until golden brown.
10. Repeat the process until all the batter has been used.
11. Serve immediately, each crumpet spread with a large knob of butter.

Eccles cakes are wonderful pastry puffs filled with spiced buttered currants which originated in Eccles in Lancashire. First made in the late eighteenth century by the baker James Birch, they are considered to be a reinvention of the earlier Banbury cake, much loved by the Tudors and traditionally sold on religious holidays.

SPICED ECCLES CAKES

Served warm for maximum pleasure, Eccles cakes are the perfect companion for Lancashire cheese, perhaps with a cup of whisky-laced tea.

I always buy the puff pastry as it is a bit of a fiddle to make and commercial brands are very good.

MAKES ABOUT 12

75g/3oz golden caster sugar
50g/2oz salted butter
½ teaspoon ground cinnamon
¼ teaspoon ground nutmeg

¼ teaspoon ground allspice
225g/8oz currants
25g/1oz candied peel
500g/1lb 2oz puff pastry

1. Preheat the oven to 220ºC /425ºF/gas mark 7.
2. Melt the sugar and butter in a heavy-based pan; stir in the spices, followed by the currants and candied peel.
3. Roll out the puff pastry, on a floured surface, until fairly thin and cut into 10cm/4in rounds.
4. Divide the currant mixture equally between the discs of pastry. To assemble the puffs first dampen the edges with a little water before folding them in and pinching together until sealed. Turn over and carefully flatten with a rolling pin until the currants just start to show.
5. Place the cakes on a baking tray, brush each cake with a little water and sprinkle with some extra sugar. Finish by cutting 3 short slits across the top of each cake.
6. Place on the middle shelf of the oven for 15 minutes, and they will blossom into beautiful puffs.

JAM TARTS

Jam tarts are the Queen of Hearts' favourite tea party treat (and the Knave of Hearts', too!) in the nursery rhyme. You can simply serve them filled with jam or lemon, or adorn them with thick whipped cream and soft fruits for a showier, more sophisticated effect.

For the perfect cheat's recipe buy sweet shortcrust pastry, but it is imperative to use good jam if you don't want to be found out.

MAKES ABOUT 12 TARTS
The basic tart:
200g/7oz sweet shortcrust pastry
home-made jam or lemon curd

For something more special:
200ml/ 7floz double cream, whipped until thick
fruit to decorate – I like to use champagne and strawberry jam (see page 41) topped with cream and halved fresh strawberries or lemon curd decorated with whipped cream mixed with a little lemon zest.

1. Preheat the oven to 200°C/400°F/gas mark 6 and grease a tart tray.
2. On a lightly floured surface roll out the pastry, cut rounds with a fluted pastry cutter, then gently press into the prepared tart tray.
3. Add a teaspoon of good jam or lemon curd into each pastry case and bake for 10 minutes.
4. Either serve plain, hot from the oven, or allow to cool and decorate with the whipped cream, using a piping bag, and fruit of your choice.

COFFEE AND WALNUT CAKE

The wonderful old-fashioned coffee and walnut cake is the perfect centrepiece to a vintage tea. Both my grandmother and my mother always baked this cake for Sunday afternoon tea and I relish every opportunity to continue the tradition.

175g/6oz soft unsalted butter
175g/6oz caster sugar
3 medium free-range eggs
1 tablespoon strong espresso coffee or
    2 teaspoons instant coffee dissolved in 1 tablespoon warm water
175g/6oz self-raising flour, sifted
60g/2½oz walnuts, chopped
A handful of walnut halves to decorate

Buttercream icing
125g/4½oz soft unsalted butter
200g/7oz icing sugar
1 tablespoon strong espresso coffee or
    2 teaspoons instant coffee dissolved in 1 tablespoon warm water

1. Preheat the oven to 190°C/375°F/gas mark 5.
2. Line 2 x 20cm/8in cake tins with greaseproof paper.
3. Beat the butter and sugar together until pale in colour and fluffy in texture.
4. Beat in the eggs one by one, then beat in the coffee.
5. Fold in the sifted flour and the chopped walnuts.
6. Divide the mixture equally between the cake tins and bake in the middle of the oven for 25 minutes, or until the cake springs back when lightly touched.
7. Remove from the oven and when cool enough to touch turn out on to a cake rack.
8. Meanwhile make the buttercream by beating the soft butter and icing sugar together; when light and fluffy beat in the coffee.

9. Place one of the cakes on a cake stand and spread with half the buttercream, put the other cake on top and cover with the remaining buttercream, and decorate with walnut halves.

DATE AND WALNUT CAKE

This is the perfect cake for a cold winter afternoon. Serve with a good strong cup of Assam tea.

200g/7oz self-raising flour
110g/4oz soft butter
75g/3oz chopped dates
25g/1oz chopped walnuts

75g/3oz soft light brown sugar
2 medium free-range eggs
125ml/5floz milk

1. Preheat the oven to 190ºC/375ºF/gas mark 5 and line a loaf tin with greaseproof paper.
2. Sift the flour into a large bowl, then rub in the softened butter until breadcrumbs form.
3. Add the dates, walnuts and sugar, and mix well.
4. Beat the eggs and milk together, then stir into the flour mixture until well incorporated.
5. Spoon the mixture into the prepared loaf tin and cook on the middle shelf of the oven for about 1¼ hours, or until the cake springs back when lightly touched in the middle.
6. Remove from the oven, then when cool enough to touch, turn the cake out, peel off the greaseproof paper and allow to cool on a wire rack. Serve in thick slices preferably spread with unsalted butter.

GREEN TEA TODDY

Green tea toddy — a warming cup of honey, whisky, lemon and green tea to serve by the fire. Of course some guests may prefer a stiffer drink than others, so have all the ingredients to hand and mix to individual tastes at the table in the old-fashioned way.

Make a pot of green tea and squeeze some lemons (the amount will depend on how many people you are entertaining).

Pour the tea into tea glasses, then add whisky, honey and fresh lemon juice to taste.

ASSAM TEA WITH RUM OR WHISKEY

Assam tea is a sturdy brew that you can stand a spoon up in. For any high tea make a good strong pot of Assam tea and simply serve it with milk, rum or Irish whiskey and sugar and enjoy.

TEA IN THE GARDEN

There is nothing quite like the first sunny summer's day when you can dust the cobwebs from the garden furniture and turn your thoughts to tea in the garden. Wafer-thin cucumber sandwiches, Victoria sponge decked with sugared rose petals and the fête favourites, butterfly cakes, are perfect summery fare. And there have to be meringues, served with lusciously ripe raspberries, buttered bread spread with rose petal jam (see page 39), and Earl Grey tea or maybe an indulgent champagne cup (see page 59).

Place the table in a shady spot, cover with a lace cloth and lay with the prettiest china in the cupboard. Adorn with cake stands and roses. Or for a long languid afternoon, simply re-create a Devon cream tea with warm home-made scones, thickly spread with jam and cream, and a bowl of sweet strawberries. You can follow up with a doze in a deckchair before supper.

WATERCRESS AND TOMATO SANDWICHES

Served on rye bread these sandwiches are so simple and delicious – the taste of summer in a single bite. Only use the tastiest, sweetest tomatoes you can find. I like to use rye bread with sunflower seeds for added texture.

First peel the tomatoes: place them in a bowl and cover with boiling water to split the skins, then pour off the water and peel away the skins with the help of a small knife. Thinly slice and place on a plate covered with a sheet of kitchen paper to remove any excess water.

Butter rye bread with softened salted butter, cover half with the tomato slices and sprinkle with a little sea salt and freshly ground black pepper. Top with watercress and press the remaining buttered slices of bread on top. With a sharp knife, remove the crusts and cut into fingers.

THE PERFECT CUCUMBER SANDWICH

No afternoon tea is complete without the quintessentially English cucumber sandwich. The ingredients may seem simple but there is an art to making the perfect sandwich. The cucumber must be firm, the bread thinly cut and the sandwich made as near to serving as possible.

Peel the cucumber with a vegetable peeler; then, with a sharp knife, cut it into wafer-thin slices. Arrange in a sieve and sprinkle with fine sea salt. Leave for 20 minutes or so, then shake off any excess water. Transfer the slices to a plate lined with kitchen paper and pat dry with another sheet. This is a bit of an effort, but it's worth it, as otherwise the bread will become soggy.

Meanwhile slice brown bread as thinly as possible and butter with soft salted butter. Cover the bread with 2 layers of cucumber, sprinkle with freshly ground black pepper, then gently press a buttered slice of bread on top. Cut off the crusts and cut into dainty fingers or triangles.

The sandwiches dry out quite quickly so either store in a sealed container until serving or cover with a damp tea towel.

BUTTERFLY CAKES WITH VANILLA BUTTERCREAM

These dainty little cakes, filled with vanilla buttercream and topped with cake 'butterfly wings', are a staple of village fêtes and the Women's Institute cake stall.

MAKES 12

110g/4oz soft butter
110g/4oz caster sugar
2 medium free-range eggs
1 teaspoon vanilla extract
110g/4oz self-raising flour

Buttercream
110g/4oz soft butter
175g/6oz icing sugar, sifted
I vanilla pod
1 tablespoon milk

1. Preheat the oven to 180°C/350°F/gas mark 4.
2. Place 12 paper cake cases in the indents of a twelve-hole tart tray.
3. Cream the butter and sugar together until very light and fluffy.
4. Beat each egg separately into the butter mixture, then beat in the vanilla extract.
5. Fold in the flour until well mixed.
6. Spoon the cake mixture into the paper cake cases until two-thirds full.
7. Bake on the middle shelf of the oven for 15–18 minutes, until golden brown and firm to the touch when gently pressed. Remove from the oven and allow to cool.
8. Meanwhile make the buttercream: beat the butter and sifted icing sugar together until very light and creamy, beat in the milk and finally the seeds scraped from inside the vanilla pod.
9. Using a sharp knife, cut a 2cm/1in circle from the centre of each cake. Cut the circle of cake in half to make 'butterfly wings'.
10. Fill each hole with buttercream, then place the 'wings' on top. Finally dust with sifted icing sugar.

With the advent of the railways, city dwellers started to take day trips into the countryside. No day out could be complete without somewhere to take tea, prompting enterprising rural folk to open their gardens and serve afternoon tea. Thus the ritual of the English cream tea was born.

BUTTERMILK SCONES

I think these are best served warm from the oven, split in half, spread with a dollop of home-made jam or lemon curd, and topped with clotted cream or thick double cream. But if you prefer to simply butter your scone you might like to add 50g/2oz of any dried fruit at the same time as the sugar.

MAKES ABOUT 12

225g/8oz self-raising flour
½ teaspoon baking powder
40g/1½oz caster sugar

75g/3oz soft butter, cut into small cubes
2 tablespoons buttermilk or milk
1 medium free-range egg, beaten

To serve
home-made jam or lemon curd
clotted or whipped double cream

1. Preheat the oven to 220°C/425°F/gas mark 7.
2. Sift the flour and baking powder into a bowl and stir in the sugar. Add the butter and rub together using your fingers until breadcrumbs form. Make a well in the centre.
3. Beat the buttermilk with the egg and pour into the well, stirring together until a light spongy dough forms that is just firm enough to handle. Do not overwork the dough or it will become tough.
4. Turn out the dough on to a very lightly floured surface and gently roll out until 2.5cm/1in thick.
5. Cut into rounds using a 5cm/2in cutter, place on a baking tray and bake, near to the top of the oven for 10–12 minutes, until golden brown and well risen.

GINGER BRANDY SNAPS WITH CARDAMOM CREAM

Brandy snaps, traditionally known as fairings, originated as a sweet treat sold at fairs in medieval times. Crunchy, lacy and spiced with ginger, they form the perfect container for piped cardamom cream.

I always make them in 2 batches so they have enough space to spread on the baking tray and so that I have time to roll them before they cool too much and become brittle.

MAKES 10

55g/2oz butter
55g/2oz demerara sugar
55g/2oz golden syrup
1 teaspoon ground ginger

55g/2oz plain flour
½ teaspoon lemon juice
150ml /¼ pint double cream
¼ teaspoon ground cardamom seeds

1. Preheat the oven to 200°C/400°F/gas mark 6.
2. Gently warm the butter, sugar, golden syrup and ground ginger in a heavy-bottomed saucepan until the sugar has melted and a syrup has formed.
3. Remove from the heat and stir in the flour and lemon juice.
4. Drop 5 teaspoons of the mixture on to a greased baking tray, leaving enough space between dollops for the brandy snaps to double in size.
5. Bake in the oven for 15 minutes until they become golden in colour and lacy in texture.
6. Lift the brandy snaps and fold them around the handle of a wooden spoon to form a curl. While still warm they bend easily into shape; as they cool they become hard and crunchy.
7. Repeat the whole process with the remaining mixture.
8. Whip the cream and stir in the ground cardamom seeds. Then pipe the cream into the cooled brandy snaps.

Meringues, so aptly called sugar puffs in the seventeenth century, are suitably light and dainty for a summer tea in the garden. Historically, egg whites would have been beaten with birch sticks, and caraway seeds or ground almond added for extra flavour.

MERINGUES WITH RASPBERRIES AND ROSE CREAM

This is the perfect combination of flavours. Add the rose water gradually to the whipped cream until you reach the desired taste for your palate.

MAKES 16

3 large free-range egg whites
175g/6oz caster sugar
275ml/½ pint double cream

rose water
small punnet of ripe raspberries

1. Preheat the oven to 110°C/225°F/gas mark ¼.
2. Line a baking tray with greaseproof paper.
3. In a large bowl whisk the egg whites, until very stiff.
4. Gradually add the sugar, whisking constantly until the surface of the meringue is glossy and thick in texture.
5. Dollop dessertspoons of the mixture on to the prepared baking tray, leaving enough space to allow them to spread a little.
6. Bake on the low shelf of the oven for 1 hour until crisp and easily lifted off the greaseproof paper; if they're too soft, cook for a further 15 minutes.
7. Whip the double cream until thick, then fold in the desired amount of rose water.
8. When the meringues are cool, sandwich with the whipped cream and decorate with raspberries.

VICTORIA SANDWICH CAKE WITH ROSE PETAL JAM AND SUGARED ROSE PETALS

The classic teatime cake is said to have been created for Queen Victoria, who adored tea parties and all things sweet. My grandmother always mixed rose petal jam (see page 39) with raspberry jam to give a slightly scented flavour to the filling.

Sugared rose petals (see page 100) make the perfect decoration.

225g/8oz soft butter
225g/8oz caster sugar
1 teaspoon vanilla extract
4 medium free-range eggs
225g/8oz self-raising flour, sifted
2 tablespoons raspberry jam mixed with 2 flat tablespoons rose petal jam
300ml/½ pint double cream, whipped until thick
icing sugar to dust
sugared rose petals to decorate

1. Preheat the oven to 190ºC/375ºF/gas mark 5.
2. Line 2 x 20cm/8in cake tins with greaseproof paper.
3. Cream the butter and sugar together until the mixture is very pale and fluffy.
4. Add the vanilla extract.
5. Beat in each egg individually, making sure each is well incorporated before adding the next. It is really worth taking the time to do this.
6. Fold in the sifted flour with a metal spoon.
7. Divide the mixture equally between the two lined tins and smooth with a knife.
8. Place the cakes on the middle shelf of the oven and bake for 20–25 minutes, or until the cakes are golden brown and the tops spring back when lightly pressed in the middle.
9. Allow the cakes to cool in the tins for 5 minutes, then turn out on a cake rack and remove the greaseproof paper.

10. When the cakes are cool put one of them on a cake stand and spread with the raspberry and rose petal jam, then cover with the whipped double cream.
11. Dust the remaining cake with sifted icing sugar and carefully place on top of the cream.
12. Decorate with the sugared rose petals.

ENGLISH MADELEINES

These conical coconut-and-jam-covered light sponges were so much a part of my childhood teas that every time I taste them I have a Proust moment and am transported back in time. Quite different from French madeleines, they look incredibly striking on the tea table.

MAKES 10

110g/4oz soft butter
110g/4oz caster sugar
2 medium free-range eggs
110g/4oz self-raising flour, sifted

seedless raspberry jam
fine desiccated coconut
5 glacé cherries, halved

1. Preheat the oven to 190°C/375°F/gas mark 5.
2. Grease 10 dariole moulds with butter and dust with a little flour.
3. Cream the butter and sugar together until light and fluffy and pale in colour.
4. Beat in each egg separately.
5. Fold in the flour until well mixed.
6. Fill the dariole moulds until three-quarters full and place on a baking tray.
7. Bake on the middle shelf of the oven for 15–20 minutes until golden brown and firm to the touch.
8. Remove from the oven and allow to cool for 5 minutes or so, then carefully turn out with the help of a thin knife on to a cooling rack.
9. When cool cut the bottoms with a sharp knife so they stand straight and at the same height.
10. Melt some raspberry jam in a saucepan and brush it over the madeleines with a pastry brush. Roll them in the desiccated coconut, then finish by dipping half a glacé cherry in the jam and placing on top.

SUGARED ROSE PETALS

This really simple recipe produces the perfect decoration for any cake.

Collect your rose petals, making sure they are pesticide- and insect-free. Lightly whip a little egg white and paint this over the surface of the petals. Place the petals on a cake rack and dust with icing sugar.

Allow the petals to dry before decorating your cake.

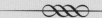

EARL GREY TEA WITH GIN AND LEMON

A delicious teatime cocktail. I always make a big pot of Earl Grey tea, then play around with the ingredients to make my perfect mix or to suit the tastes of my guests. Serve in teacups with saucers. Ice the Earl Grey tea for a summer garden party.

gin
pot of Earl Grey tea, freshly brewed or iced
freshly squeezed lemon juice, served in a milk jug
caster sugar, in a sugar bowl
unwaxed lemon slices

Pour a good slug of gin into a teacup, pour in the freshly brewed Earl Grey tea, then add a little freshly squeezed lemon juice and caster sugar to taste. Stir until the sugar is dissolved, and serve with a slice of lemon.

FIRESIDE TEA

*O*n dark winter evenings there is nothing more comforting than serving afternoon tea around a roaring fire.

Toasted muffins, crumpets and currant buns are top of the menu for a fireside tea. If you have a toasting fork your guests can do the toasting for themselves; a toaster is a less fun, though perhaps more practical, alternative.

Hot buttered toast served with potted salmon (see page 69) is an old-fashioned savoury treat. For those with a sweet tooth simply sprinkle the toast with cinnamon sugar or spread with home-made jam. A slice of rich fruitcake or Madeira cake with a warming hot toddy will ward off the cold.

There is no need to lay a formal table; instead just cover a wooden tray with a cloth and pile high with treats. Find the comfiest chair and, with a napkin at hand, dig in.

CINNAMON SUGAR

Mix equal amounts of ground cinnamon and golden caster sugar, and sprinkle on anything hot, toasted and buttered.

TOAST

Much loved since the Middle Ages, toast is the great English speciality, and perfect for a winter tea. An open fire is simply crying out to be used to make toast, so arm yourself with a toasting fork and have a go.

Toast is best made with day-old bread and must be eaten immediately whilst hot, and still crunchy on the outside and soft on the inside. Enjoy the aroma as you smother it with butter.

Toast is adaptable, so top with sweet things – jam, honey or cinnamon sugar – or with savoury – potted salmon, anchovies, cheese or even Marmite mixed with butter. Get spreading!

CHEESE, APPLE AND WALNUT SANDWICHES

Mix grated cheddar cheese, grated apple and chopped walnuts with mayonnaise for a tasty winter sandwich filling.

By the mid-nineteenth century muffins were so popular that they were sold in the streets at teatime by bell-ringing muffin men. At the height of their popularity there were so many sellers trying to out-ring each other that the streets became unbearably noisy, causing the use of the bell to be banned by Act of Parliament.

Etiquette books gave instructions on how muffins should be eaten: toast each side on a toasting fork over an open fire, never cut open with a knife, simply prise apart, place a large knob of butter between the two halves and gently press together, allowing the butter to melt into the muffin before you eat it.

If you are the proud owner of a muffin dish ingeniously designed to maintain your muffin at the perfect temperature, use it with a flourish.

ENGLISH MUFFINS

Muffins are soft and spongy on the inside and crunchy on the outside, and made from yeasted dough cooked on a hot griddle. Prise each one open around the edge with your fingers and then tear (never cut) into two halves.

MAKES 12

450g/1lb strong plain flour
1 teaspoon salt
150ml/6fl oz milk

110ml/4fl oz water
1 teaspoon caster sugar
2 teaspoons dried yeast

1. Sift the flour and salt into a large bowl and make a well in the centre.
2. Warm the milk and water until hand hot, remove from the heat and pour into a bowl; stir in the sugar and dried yeast until dissolved. Leave in a warm place for about 10 minutes, or until the mixture has become very frothy.
3. Pour it into the well in the flour and mix together until a soft dough forms.
4. Knead the dough for 10 minutes, then cover with a cloth and leave in a warm place until it has doubled in size; this will take about 45 minutes.
5. Carefully cut the dough into 12 pieces and shape into 7cm/3in rounds, gently flattened with the palm of your hand.
6. Place on a floured board, cover with a cloth and allow to rise for a further 25 minutes.
7. Heat a griddle or a heavy-based frying pan to a moderate temperature. Cook the muffins, in three batches, for about 7 minutes on each side; the muffins will become golden brown but will still remain white around the edge.
8. Serve immediately, torn apart and spread with as much butter as you dare; if the muffins have cooled, lightly toast them whole.

The unique two-tone Battenberg cake was said to have been designed in 1884 to commemorate the marriage of Queen Victoria's granddaughter, Princess Victoria of Hesse, to Louis of Battenberg. Its alternating squares of pink and yellow sponge wrapped in almond paste may have been inspired by the marbled appearance typical of the German cakes in Louis's homeland.

BATTENBERG CAKE

This pretty, retro cake will impress all your guests with its 16 little squares rather than the more usual 4.
     You will need 2 x 20cm/8in by 12cm/5in (approx.) loaf tins.

225g/8oz soft unsalted butter
225g/8oz caster sugar
4 medium free-range eggs
275g/10oz self-raising flour, sifted
pink food colouring
seedless raspberry jam,
     warmed gently in a pan

Almond paste
150g/5oz ground almonds
55g/2oz caster sugar
75g/3oz icing sugar
1 teaspoon lemon juice
1 large free-range egg, beaten

1. Preheat the oven to 190°C/ 375°F/gas mark 5.
2. Line the loaf tins with greaseproof paper.
3. Beat the butter and sugar until light and fluffy.
4. Beat in each egg individually.
5. Fold in the sifted flour.
6. Divide the mixture into two halves. Place one half into one tin; add a little pink food colouring into the remaining mixture, then fill the second tin.
7. Place on the middle shelf of the oven and bake for 30–35 minutes until the cake springs back when lightly pressed in the middle.
8. When cool enough to touch turn out the cakes, peel off the paper and allow to cool on a cake rack.

9. With a sharp knife trim off the outside edges of the cake, then cut each cake lengthwise into 4 strips, then again in half to form 8 long cuboids of cake.

10. Brush each surface of the cake sections with the warm raspberry jam; this will glue them together as you arrange them alternately in colour, 4 to each side, making a chequered effect.

11. Sift the dry almond paste ingredients into a bowl; add the lemon juice and enough beaten egg to bind together, and knead to form a thick paste.

12. Roll out the paste until it is the same length as the cake and wide enough to cover it with a little overlap. Brush the paste with the warm jam, place the cake in the centre and tightly wrap the paste around, gently pushing the edges together to seal. Trim away any excess paste from the ends and place on a plate with the join underneath.

CURRANT BUNS

No fireside tea is complete without the currant bun or tea cake. Sweet, yeasted fruit buns were the forerunner of cake (before the discovery that whisked eggs could serve as a raising agent).

MAKES 12

275ml/½ pint milk, warmed
1 tablespoon dried yeast
75g/3oz caster sugar, plus 1 teaspoon
450g/1lb strong plain flour, sifted
50g/2oz butter, melted

75g/3oz currants
25g/1oz mixed peel
1 teaspoon of caster sugar dissolved in
2 tablespoons of milk to glaze

1. Preheat the oven to 200°C/400°F/gas mark 6.
2. Heat half of the milk until hand warm, pour into a jug and stir in the dried yeast and 1 teaspoon of the sugar; set to one side until the mixture becomes frothy.
3. Sift the flour into a bowl and stir in the remaining sugar. Make a well in its centre and pour in the yeast mix, the remaining milk and the melted butter. Mix together and knead to form a firm dough.
4. Knead in the dried fruit and peel, then cover with a cloth and set to one side in a warm place until the dough has risen to double its original size (this should take about an hour).
5. Knead a little again, then cut into 12 pieces, form into little buns and place on a greased baking tray. Cover with a cloth and leave for a further 30 minutes.
6. Brush with the glaze and bake for about 20 minutes until golden brown. Serve warm from the oven or toasted, and spread with lashings of butter.

MADEIRA CAKE

This dense buttery cake, instantly recognizable by its citron peel topping, is a teatime classic. The cake mixture was also used as a base for seed cake and rich cherry cake, so feel free to add 2 teaspoons caraway seeds or 75g/3oz halved and rinsed glacé cherries to the cake mixture, in place of the lemon zest and candied peel, and bake in a loaf tin.

If citron peel is hard to find, simply simmer strips of lemon peel in a sugar solution (1 tablespoon caster sugar to 3 tablespoons water) until translucent.

Why not serve your cake in vintage style, with a glass of Madeira?

150g/5oz soft butter
150g/5oz caster sugar
3 large free-range eggs
225g/8oz self-raising flour
grated zest of a lemon
2 tablespoons or so of milk to mix
4 x 1.5cm/½in thick strips of candied or citron peel
caster sugar to decorate

1. Line a 18cm/7in loose-bottomed cake tin with greaseproof paper and preheat the oven to170°C/325°F/gas mark 3.
2. Cream the butter and sugar together until light and fluffy.
3. Beat in each egg, individually, then fold in the flour, lemon zest and milk.
4. Spoon the mixture into the prepared tin and carefully lay the citron peel on top; don't push the peel down or it will sink as the cake rises.
5. Bake on the middle shelf of the preheated oven for 1¼ hours, or until the cake feels firm in the middle.
6. Remove from the oven and dust with caster sugar while still warm.

During the eighteenth century the use of yeast (originally taken from the top of beer) as a raising agent in cakes was replaced after the discovery of the leavening power of beaten eggs. This heralded the birth of the superb sponge cake. Recipes of the time would instruct the cook to beat the eggs for literally hours. Madeira cake is the classic example of the new method and was taken as a mid-morning snack served with its namesake, the fortified wine Madeira.

The Dundee cake was created at the end of the nineteenth century by Keiller's, the famous Scottish marmalade maker, as an ingenious way to use up any spare citrus peel left over during the months when marmalade was not produced. The recipe was kept firmly secret but, although there was a strict gentleman's agreement in Scotland that no one else would manufacture the cake, it did not stop the English having a try.

DUNDEE CAKE

Winter afternoon tea calls for a good fruitcake and the rich, buttery Dundee cake with its topping of blanched almonds and cherries fits the bill. Like Christmas cake, it keeps incredibly well, so I always make two smaller cakes, which look very elegant, and on a practical level this shortens the baking time.

225g/8oz plain flour
1 teaspoon baking powder
¼ teaspoon salt
175g/6oz soft butter
150g/5oz caster sugar
3 medium free-range eggs
175g/6oz sultanas
110g/4oz currants
50g/2oz mixed peel,
    cut small with a knife

50g/2oz glacé cherries,
    washed dried and cut in half
grated zest of an orange
grated zest of a lemon
50g/2oz ground almonds
milk to mix
blanched whole almonds to decorate
marmalade to glaze

1. Preheat the oven to 170°C/325°F/gas mark 3.
2. Line a 20cm/8in or 2 x 10cm/4in loose-bottomed cake tins with greaseproof paper.
3. Sift the flour, baking powder and salt together.
4. Beat the butter and sugar together until light and fluffy.
5. Beat in each egg individually.

6. Fold in the flour, baking powder and salt mixture.
7. Fold in the fruit, peel, cherries, grated zest and ground almonds. The mixture should have a stiff dropping consistency so add a little milk if necessary.
8. Turn the mixture into the prepared tin.
9. Lightly arrange the blanched almonds in concentric circles on the top of the cake (don't press too hard or they will sink).
10. Bake on the middle shelf of the oven for 1½ to 2 hours (1¼ if making smaller cakes), or until the cake springs back when pressed lightly in the middle.
11. When cool enough to handle, remove from the tin and allow to cool on a wire rack.
12. Melt a little marmalade and brush it over the top of the cake.

ROSEHIP SYRUP WITH VODKA AND SODA

When I was a child, autumn always signalled the appearance of rosehip syrup; my mother considered it protection against colds as it is full of vitamin C. In late summer we would help pick rosy red hips from the garden and always used to carry a bag with us when walking to collect hips from wild briar roses. Later, I discovered how delicious the syrup is mixed with vodka! Why not maintain tradition and serve your guests a 'healthy' winter cocktail? Simply mix to taste with vodka, top with soda, and garnish with fresh mint leaves.

The syrup recipe is for 1kg (2.2lb) of rosehips but make as much or as little as you like using the same proportion of fruit to sugar. I always bottle the liquid in small amounts, as it does not keep very long once open.

TO MAKE THE ROSEHIP SYRUP
1kg/2.2lb rosehips
2½ litres/4½ pints water
500g/.1.1 lb white granulated sugar
jelly bag or muslin square

1. Top and tail the rosehips and give them a good wash.
2. Bring two-thirds of the water to boil in a pan large enough to fit the rosehips.
3. Roughly chop the rosehips in a food processor, then add to the boiling water; bring back to the boil, then remove from the heat, cover and leave for half an hour or so.
4. Strain the mixture through a jelly bag or muslin-lined sieve, squeeze the bag to remove all liquid and set to one side.
5. Return the pulp to the pan with the remaining water and bring to the boil, set aside for a further half an hour, then strain again.
6. Combine all the strained liquid in a clean pan, bring to the boil, then simmer until the liquid has reduced by half.
7. Pour in the sugar, stir until dissolved, then bring to a rapid boil for 5 minutes.
8. Decant into warm sterilized bottles and seal immediately.

NURSERY TEA

*W*hen children were seen but not heard, tea was served in the nursery and there were many strictures: bread and butter had to be eaten before cake, sardine sandwiches were considered nutritious, jam was a treat, and cakes were modest.

Now the old-fashioned nursery tea can be much more fun! Serve Marmite and jam sandwiches cut into pretty shapes, hot drop scones with butter and honey, jam tarts and jammy biscuits, pretty English madeleines (see page 99) and colourful little iced cakes.

Naturally, dolls and teddies are honoured guests who deserve their own tea set.

MINI NURSERY CAKES

MAKES 12 CAKES

Make the cakes as described in the lemon drops recipe (see page 46) until you reach the point when you have cut out the little cakes.

Make glacé icing by gradually adding a little water to 110g/4oz icing sugar until a smooth thick icing is formed. You can add food colouring at this point to create different-coloured icing if you wish.

Carefully spread icing on each cake and top with a coloured sugared jelly.

JAMMY BISCUITS

Jammy biscuits are always a firm favourite on the nursery tea table. Follow the shortbread recipe on page 57 for a yummy biscuit base.

Roll out the dough to ½cm/ thick and cut into shapes; hearts work well and look pretty. Place the biscuits on a non-stick baking tray; then, using the handle of a wooden spoon, make an indent in the middle of each biscuit. Fill with whichever jam takes your fancy, then bake as instructed in the recipe.

SWISS ROLL

To make a classic jam Swiss roll, make a Genoese cake as on page 58. Turn out the cake slab on to a sheet of greaseproof paper generously sprinkled with caster sugar.

Cut a groove into the short nearside end of the cake about 1cm/½in away from the edge; this will help you start to roll the cake.

Spread with jam of your choice; then, pulling the greaseproof paper up to help you, tightly roll the cake. Dust with a little more caster sugar and serve in slices with cream and soft fruit.

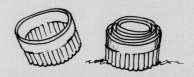

DROP SCONES

These tiny thick pancakes, made from a thick batter and cooked on a griddle pan, are best eaten whilst still hot, straight from the pan, smothered with butter and honey.

MAKES ABOUT 20

225g/8oz plain flour
½ teaspoon bicarbonate of soda
½ teaspoon cream of tartar
pinch of salt

2 medium free-range eggs
25g/1oz caster sugar
275ml/½ pint milk

1. Sift the flour, bicarbonate of soda, cream of tartar and salt into a bowl.
2. Beat the eggs and sugar together, then gradually beat in the milk; pour into the flour mixture and mix until all the ingredients are incorporated to form a thick smooth, slightly bubbly batter.
3. Heat an oiled griddle or heavy-based frying pan to a moderate temperature; drop dessertspoons of the mixture on to the griddle, leaving enough space for them to spread. You will need to do this in a few batches. Turn the scones when the bubbles burst, and cook for a further few minutes until the scones are golden brown.
4. Remove from the griddle and cover with a pretty cloth until ready to serve.

Until the coal-fired range came into use, in the nineteenth century, the griddle was the most common home-baking device – hence the early proliferation of recipes such as drop scones, muffins and crumpets. Anything that needed oven-baking had to be either sent out to the local bakehouse or done in unpredictable wood burning stoves. A roaring fire would be built up in the morning. All the quick cooking, high-temperature baking would be done first, then as the temperature dropped during the day the slower-cooking recipes would be made. All this would be done on one day – baking day! The arrival of the new-fangled range-style coal oven with its excellent heat control allowed more creative baking.

INDEX OF RECIPES